I. Introduction

Economists have long believed that, other things equal, increases in market concentration reduce competition. In turn, less competitive markets lead to higher consumer prices and reduce consumer welfare. This belief provides the basis for much of the world's antitrust policy. The U.S., U.K. and E.U., for example, review mergers prospectively. While each agency operates in a different legal environment, the economic logic underlying merger review is the same. Horizontal mergers can create or enhance market power by combining firms producing substitute products.[1] The problem for regulators is determining which mergers are likely to result in reduced competition. Unfortunately, there is remarkably little reliable systematic evidence linking measures of market concentration such as the Herfindahl-Hirschman Index (HHI) to manufacturer markups or consumer prices.[2]

Empirically identifying a causal relationship between price and market concentration is extremely difficult because market concentration is rarely exogenously determined. Demsetz (1973) noted firms that attain large market shares are likely those that are most efficient, and that markets where scale economies are important will tend to be dominated by a small number of efficient firms. As a result, studies that simply estimate the price/concentration relationship without controlling for the endogeneity of market structure are unlikely to be successful (Evans et al. (1993)), Bresnahan and Reiss (1989, 1990)).

In this paper we estimate the relationship between consumer prices and market structure by examining how prices change following significant changes in market structure resulting from horizontal mergers in the supermarket industry. Like other retail industries, the supermarket

---

[1] See Section 1 of the 2010 U.S. Department of Justice(DOJ)/Federal Trade Commission (FTC) *Horizontal Merger Guidelines* for a clear description of the economic logic underlying U.S. horizontal merger policy.
[2] The Herfindahl-Hirschman Index is defined as the sum of the squared market shares of market participants, where firm's market shares are typically measured as percentage points.

industry is often viewed as one in which entry and expansion should be relatively easy. Assuming a retailer has an existing supply network, it need only identify an effective location and obtain permission from local regulators to open an establishment. The sunk costs of entry (e.g., the cost of structures and permits), in particular, are likely much lower than in most industries. Overall, the industry appears to be quite competitive with estimated net post-tax profit margins of only 1.37% over the last decade.[3] Notwithstanding the perceived ease of entry and expansion in the industry and relatively low profit margins, mergers in retail markets are often subject to material antitrust review. Between 1998 and 2007, for example, the FTC investigated supermarket mergers affecting 153 antitrust markets and challenged mergers in 134 of those markets.[4] Surprisingly, given this enforcement focus, we are aware of only one study that has estimated the price effects of a consummated horizontal merger in this industry.[5]

We infer causality using two related empirical techniques. We begin by conducting a standard difference-in-difference analysis: we compare prices in markets experiencing a merger to those in similar markets not experiencing a major change in market structure resulting from entry, exit, or a horizontal merger. The major criticism of this method is that the decision to merge may be related to market participants' expectations about future prices in an industry resulting in biased price effects (Nevo and Whinston (2010)). To address this concern we examine the robustness of our findings to the choice of comparison group and also estimate price effects using the synthetic control group approach suggested by Abadie et al. (2010).

---

[3] Food Marketing Institute estimates of grocery store chain's net profits, available at: http://www.fmi.org/docs/facts-figures/net-profit-percent-sales-2011.pdf?sfvrsn=2, last visited November 6th, 2012.
[4] Horizontal Merger Investigation Data, Fiscal Years 1996-2007, Federal Trade Commission, Table 4-2. Available at http://www.ftc.gov/os/2008/12/081201hsrmergerdata.pdf.
[5] Huang and Stiegert (2009) estimate the price effects of the merger of grocery retailers Kohls and Copps in Madison, Wisconsin. They find that while the merger did not result in a price increase in the months immediately following the merger, the merged firms' prices had risen relative to the control market two years later.

Overall, our results are supportive of the hypothesis that increases in market concentration resulting from mergers cause prices to increase when mergers take place in already concentrated markets. In analyzing horizontal mergers, antitrust agencies look at the level and change in market concentration associated with a merger as a predictor of competitive harm. The 2010 *Horizontal Merger Guidelines*, for example, state that "Mergers in highly concentrated markets [markets with an HHI greater than 2500] that involve an increase in the HHI of more than 200 points will be presumed to be likely to enhance market power."[6] In contrast, mergers in unconcentrated markets (with an HHI of less than 1500) resulting in a small change in market concentration are viewed as unlikely to be anticompetitive. In this study, we estimate the price effects of eight mergers in highly concentrated markets and six mergers in moderately concentrated or unconcentrated markets. Our results tend to confirm the presumptions of antitrust regulators as stated in the Horizontal Merger Guidelines. We find that five mergers resulted in estimated price increases of more than 2% and that four of those were in highly concentrated markets. Five mergers resulted in estimated price decreases of more than 2% and only one of those occurred in a highly concentrated market, while the remaining four mergers were associated with relatively little change in price. These findings are robust to the choice of comparison group and estimation technique.

Our paper contributes to a small but growing literature which estimates the change in price following mergers of competing firms. The goal of most papers in this literature is to measure the efficacy of antitrust enforcement. In the typical study, researchers identify mergers that were likely on the antitrust margin; that is, those mergers that the antitrust authority seriously considered challenging but allowed to go forward. If the merger resulted in a price

---

[6] The 2010 FTC/DOJ Horizontal Merger Guidelines define highly concentrated markets as those having a Herfindahl-Hirschman Index (HHI) greater than 2500. 2010 Horizontal Merger Guidelines, 5.3.

increase, the researchers conclude that policy was too lax while a price decrease indicates the regulator may be too strict (Ashenfelter et al. (2009)). The majority of these studies find that horizontal mergers increase prices. [7,8] The ability to draw general conclusions regarding the efficacy of horizontal merger policy from the published literature, however, is limited. Only a tiny fraction of the thousands of mergers filed with the U.S. antitrust agencies have been studied, and the majority of those have examined mergers in a handful of industries with a history of regulation, e.g., banking, airlines, hospitals, and petroleum. Further, most studies in this literature are case studies. While the case study methodology is often essential to credibly identify the price effects of mergers (learning and controlling for factors that affect industry pricing), the case study approach makes generalization of the finding of any one study to other situations difficult. A strength of our study, in contrast to much of the literature,[9] is that we estimate the price effects of many mergers affecting different geographic markets with different levels of market concentration at roughly the same time. In particular, we estimate the price effects of mergers in already highly concentrated markets and examine large mergers in less concentrated markets unlikely to result in a reduction in competition. By also studying mergers in less concentrated markets, we are able to examine mergers that are likely to be competitively benign but that could result in efficiencies which lower consumer prices. Our approach follows Carlton's (2009) suggestion that researchers should examine the price effects of all mergers (those likely and unlikely to result in price effects) to more fully understand how mergers affect the competitive process.

---

[7] See Weinberg (2008), Pautler (2003), and Hunter et al. (2008) for recent surveys of this literature.
[8] The major exception is the petroleum industry where the evidence is quite mixed, see Silvia and Taylor (2009) and cites therein.
[9] Prager and Hannan's (1998) study of banking mergers , Kim and Singal's (2003) study of airline mergers, and Dafny's (2009) study of hospital mergers for are notable exceptions.

The remainder of this paper is organized as follows. Section II describes our data sources, and Section III presents the methodology used to construct our merger and comparison markets. Section IV describes our estimation strategy and presents the empirical findings of the study. Section V concludes.

II. Data

Our study uses three data sources. The first is A.C. Nielsen's Trade Dimensions retail database. Each year Trade Dimensions creates a census of retail outlets operating in the U.S. for a number of retailing industries, including supermarkets, club stores, liquor stores, convenience stores, and restaurants. In this study we focus on the primary formats used for grocery retailing: conventional supermarkets, supercenters, and club stores.[10] Our dataset consists of annual observations, including the location, size, estimated sales, the store's banner (the name the store operates under), and corporate ownership of each supermarket, supercenter, and club store in the U.S. from 2004 through the fall of 2009. An additional feature of the dataset is that every store location has a unique identification number that allows us to track stores over time. For example, we can observe if a location changes ownership or if a supermarket that closes for a time reopens as a supermarket. The dataset also contains information on the ownership of different chains, which is important because many firms operate multiple retail brands, sometimes even within a relatively small geographic area. As we describe in the next section, this data allows us to identify the entry and exit of retailers from local markets and identify the merger of retailers.

---

[10] We exclude other retail formats in the Trade Dimensions Grocery dataset – limited assortment, natural/gourmet food, warehouse, and military commissary – because they are so differentiated from traditional supermarkets. For example, of these retail formats, only military commissaries offer one-stop-shopping. However, military commissaries are available to only a subset of the population.

The price data we use consists of the prices used to construct the ACCRA Cost of Living Index, which is published by the Council for Community and Economic Research (CCER). The ACCRA price index is designed to compare the cost of living for moderately affluent professional and managerial households in different U.S. metropolitan areas at a point in time.[11] The price data assembled by CCER are collected by the staffs of the roughly 350 local U.S. Chambers of Commerce who participate in the data collection project. In the first, second, and third quarter of each year, staff of participating Chambers of Commerce collect price quotes for 60 distinct products corresponding to broad categories of consumer expenditures, including housing, energy, food, transportation, and health care.[12] In this study, our primary dataset consists of the prices collected for the 26 grocery products in the ACCRA sample.[13] These prices typically correspond to a distinct food product, such as a pound of T-Bone steak or a 2 liter bottle of Coca-Cola, sold at a specific retail outlet on a given day. For the grocery items, CCER collects multiple price quotes for each item within a market at a point in time. For example, the surveyors collect multiple price quotes for 2 liter bottles of Coca-Cola in the first quarter of 2006. Smaller markets tend to have fewer price quotes per item than large markets.[14] In our data we observe the retail banner that a price quote corresponds to but not the specific retail location that was sampled. Thus, while we know that prices came from a Safeway store located in the San Francisco, CA metropolitan area in the second quarter of 2009, we do not

---

[11] See the Council's web page for more details http://www.coli.org/.
[12] As is discussed in more detail below, data collection by the individual Chambers of Commerce is voluntary. As a result, data collection does not occur in all time periods in all markets; that is, the dataset is not a balanced panel. In this study we limit our attention to those markets that have price data for at least 10 of the 14 quarters in our sample period. This restriction reduces the number of cities in our sample from 357 to 228.
[13] See Appendix A for a list of the grocery products and the expenditure weight assigned to each product.
[14] In our data we observe markets with as few as 1 retailer surveyed within a quarter while others have more than thirty. In the median market/quarter 5 retail outlets and 4 retailers are surveyed; i.e., in the median market prices two outlets of a single retailer have been visited.

know precisely which Safeway store was sampled. As a result, in our empirical analysis we must treat the broad geographic region as the geographic unit of observation.

We also use price quotes for some non-grocery items in the CCER data to control for unobserved market-specific retailing cost shocks, such as the local price of labor, that could affect grocery prices.[15] We have identified four items that are unlikely to be sold at a supermarket that would be sold at a retailer facing similar costs as a supermarket: a men's dress shirt, boy's jeans, women's slacks, and a three-pack of tennis balls. In contrast to the grocery data, we observe only a single price of these items (rather than multiple price quotes from different retailers).

The CCER data is particularly well suited to our study. First, it contains prices on a broad set of supermarket products designed to measure the typical "market basket" of consumers' food purchases. Second, the data covers more geographic regions within the U.S. than any other publicly accessible pricing data set we are aware of. This allows us to study many mergers and gives us a great deal of flexibility in identifying potential comparison cities to use in both our difference-in-difference analysis and in constructing a synthetic control. Third, we were able to collect a relatively long panel of data (5 years).

There are two key relative weaknesses of the CCER data. The first is data quality. Supermarket scanner data (often provided by A.C. Nielsen or IRI) is recorded at the supermarket and transmitted electronically to the data vendor minimizing the chance for measurement error. The U.S. Bureau of Labor Statistics (BLS) collects price quotes directly from retail outlets using trained surveyors under a strict protocol that has been developed over time to reduce measurement error. In contrast, CCER's price collection method is more informal. While

---

[15] These controls were also used by Basker and Noel (2009).

7

surveyors are given a detailed set of instructions to follow in collecting prices,[16] CCER does not enforce a formal sampling scheme. Second, the products contained in the CCER sample are, by construction, composed of frequently purchased supermarket products. As will be discussed in Section IV in more detail, the prices of frequently purchased products are more likely to be strongly affected by changes in competition than a randomly selected grocery product. As a result, the price effects of mergers we estimate likely overstate (in absolute value) the true price effect of the merger. As a practical matter, however, we have to accept somewhat lower quality data to complete our study, as the CCER is the only dataset we have been able to identify that has such broad geographic coverage for such a wide variety of grocery products.[17]

Finally, we have also obtained annual data from the Census describing the demographic characteristics of the geographic markets in which the firms compete. Demographic variables describing a region's population, income, and racial composition were collected at the county level and are aggregated to match the broad geographic regions used in this study.

III. Market Construction and Classification

Retailers are differentiated by location, by the types and quality of items sold in their stores, and by the level of service they offer consumers. As a result, market definition, identifying the geographic region in which retailers compete and the set of firms (or products) that constitute a market, can be difficult. For instance, one cannot infer different retail formats

---

[16] The instruction manual given to participants can be found at: http://www.coli.org/surveyforms/colimanual.pdf (last visited 7/17/2012).
[17] Data sets with more detailed price data have much more limited geographic coverage. The most comprehensive public use scanner dataset we are aware of, the IRI Marketing Dataset, contains the prices and unit sales of thousands of grocery products in 30 product categories for a sample of retailers, however, only provides data for 47 markets (Bronnenberg et al. 2008).[17] Another alternative data source we considered consists of the price quotes collected by the BLS in constructing the Consumer Price Index (CPI), see Hosken and Reiffen (2004a), Matsa (2011). While the CPI price data covers many more regions than the IRI Marketing Dataset (Matsa reports using data from 147 metropolitan areas), its coverage is still too narrow for our study.

are important substitutes to each other because the different retail formats sell some of the same products. Supermarkets, club stores, supercenters, convenience stores, mass-merchandisers (non-supercenter outlets operated by firms Target, Kmart, or Walmart), and drug stores, for example, all carry some food items. However, it is unlikely that all of these retail formats are similarly substitutable to one another. Convenience stores offer a very limited selection of food products in small stores at relatively high prices, while supermarkets and supercenters offer a broad selection of food products (including meat and produce) at relatively low prices in large stores. We limit our attention to the set of retail formats that are likely to significantly affect the pricing of supermarkets large grocery retailers that sell food and other household goods, e.g., cleaning products, where consumers can purchase all of their food for a week at a single retail location (often referred to as offering one-stop-shopping).[18] This limitation results in a set of retailers employing three retail formats: traditional supermarkets,[19] club stores,[20] and supercenters.[21] Even this limited set of formats, however, may be too broad. Club stores, while offering one-stop shopping, offer much more limited product selection than supermarkets or

---

[18] Recent empirical work shows that supermarkets change their prices in response to competition from supercenters and possibly club retailers suggesting that these retail formats compete with one another, see, e.g., Hausman and Liebtag (2007), Basker and Noel (2009), and Courtemanche and Carden (2011). We are unaware of empirical work that directly measures substitution between supermarkets, supercenters, club stores and other types of food retailers.

[19] A traditional supermarket is defined as a self-service retailer selling a full line of food products (including grocery, meat, and produce). See the Food Marketing Institute's Supermarket Facts available at: http://www.fmi.org/facts_figs/?fuseaction=superfact.

[20] Club stores are high volume retailers that typically charge members an annual fee and offer consumers a limited selection of a broad variety of products at lower prices than other retailers. Despite their limited product offerings (supermarkets or supercenters typically carry between 45,000 and 140,000 items while a club store may stock less than 4,000 at any point in time), club stores sell food in a large number of food categories, including meat and produce. According to Costco's 2009 Annual Report, 33% of Costco's sales were of food items with 12% of total Costco sales being Fresh Food items (including meat, bakery, deli, and produce). Given the very large sales volume of club stores (the average Costco outlet has $131 million in annual revenue), a typical club store sells more food items in a week than a very large traditional supermarket.

[21] Supercenters are an important and rapidly growing big-box grocery retail format. Supercenters are typically larger than 180,000 square feet, combining both a large supermarket and a large mass-merchandiser within the same store. The most well-known supercenter retailer, Wal-Mart, opened its first supercenter in 1988 and is now the U.S.'s largest food retailer.

supercenters, and are typically not considered important substitutes to supermarkets by antitrust agencies in evaluating supermarket mergers.[22]

Identifying the relevant geographic region that determines a store's retail prices is complicated because of spatial differentiation. Retailers have an incentive to exploit highly localized market power by charging different prices at each retail outlet in response to highly localized demand and competition. There are, however, significant costs of implementing highly localized pricing. Determining optimal prices at the store level requires retailers to invest significant resources in learning localized demand, and too much price variation across a retailer's stores within a metro area can affect a firm's ability to offer consumers a consistent price image. As a result, we observe retailers pursuing different pricing strategies within the broad markets they operate in. Ashenfelter et al. (2006) report that office supply retailer Staples changed its pricing in response to changes in competition within the broad metropolitan area in which its stores operated. In contrast, in its review of the merger of A&P and Pathmark, two large supermarket retailers with overlapping operations in the New York City and Philadelphia metropolitan areas, the FTC concluded that the merger would only adversely affect competition in two local areas within the broader New York market.[23]

In principal, we would like to estimate both how mergers affect prices within the broad geographic market affected by a merger and by analyzing prices at the individual store location. Unfortunately, like previous researchers studying competition in retail food markets (Hausman

---

[22] In its investigations of supermarket mergers the FTC has typically concluded that competition among supermarkets is primarily limited to other supermarkets. For example, the FTC's complaint challenging the merger of A&P and Pathmark in 2007 stated that: "Retail stores other than supermarkets that sell food and grocery products including neighborhood "mom & pop" grocery stores, convenience stores, specialty food stores, club stores, military commissaries, and mass merchants do not individually or collectively effectively constrain prices at supermarkets."
[23] The FTC challenged the merger of A&P/Pathmark because of concerns about localized competition in two regions within the greater New York metropolitan area (Staten Island and Shirley, New York). A&P/Pathmark satisfied the FTC's concerns by divesting 6 stores (of the 373 located in metro New York). See http://www.ftc.gov/opa/2007/11/pathwork.shtm, last visited 9/7/2012.

and Liebtag (2007), Basker and Noel (2009), Huang and Stiegert (2010)), we do not have sufficient data at the store level to estimate localized price effects. As a result, all of our empirical analysis has to be interpreted as measuring prices within the broad geographic market in which retailers compete.

Market Classification

To implement our difference-in-difference and synthetic control estimators we must identify those regions that experienced a significant change in market structure as the result of a horizontal merger (treatment markets) and those markets that experienced no significant change in market structure as the result of entry, exit, or horizontal mergers (comparison markets). We define a market as experiencing a significant change in market structure if it experiences a horizontal merger, entry, or exit affecting at least five percent of the retail outlets in the market. In our data, some markets experience a single change in market structure while others experience multiple changes in market structure (e.g., entry by a retailer and a merger). To facilitate interpretation, we only estimate the price effect of mergers for those markets whose only significant change in market structure resulted from a single merger during our sample period.

We next define two sets of potential comparison markets that we use as potential controls in the difference-in-difference and synthetic control analysis. The first consists of markets that experienced *no* change in market structure; that is, during the sample period the market experienced no entry, exit, or merger of competing firms. Because all large markets in our data experience some change in market structure (most often the entry or exit of a small chain retailer), there are no large markets in this comparison group (Hanner et al. (2011). For this reason we consider a second set of comparison markets that consists of markets that experienced a *di minimis* amount of exit, entry, or mergers: no single entry, exit, or merger event affected

11

more than 2% of stores in a market. Below we provide the technical details describing exactly how entry, exit, and mergers are defined in the study.

We define entry as a firm beginning operations as a grocery retailer in a market with a new retail brand; that is, a new firm operating in a market with a new retail brand. Our definition of entry does not include the sale of a local brand to a new firm that continues to operate retail outlets in that market under the same trade name (a new firm operating an old brand).[24] We also do not consider within market expansion – an existing retailer opening new stores of an existing banner in a market – to be entry.[25]

We define exit as an event that causes consumers to lose access to a brand *and* firm in a market. Parallel to entry, we do not view the sale of a retail brand to another corporate parent as brand exit if the subsequent owner continues to operate at least one store in an affected market under the original retail banner. Similarly, if a firm closes some but not all of the stores operating under a given banner, we consider this to be within market contraction and not exit.

In our data we observe two types of transactions that we refer to as horizontal mergers. The most common type of merger we observe occurs when one firm decides to exit a market by selling its existing operations to a current market participant. For example, in exiting the San Francisco, San Jose, and Fresno, California markets in 2007, Albertsons sold its stores to incumbent grocery retailer Save Mart Supermarkets. Save Mart then operated those store locations using a new name, Lucky. The second type of transaction is a traditional merger where an incumbent buys all of the assets of a rival. In this scenario, the acquiring firm may or may not

---

[24] Although acquisitions of this type clearly represent a change in corporate control and the entry of a new firm (rather than a brand) into a region, the set of products available to consumers (brand names of retailers) do not change as the result of the transaction.

[25] The geographic markets used in antitrust analysis are frequently more narrow than the geographic regions we have defined to be markets. As a result, what we define as a market expansion (e.g., a brand with operations in Los Angeles, California opened a store in Ventura, California) might be interpreted as market entry in an antitrust analysis (if Los Angeles and Ventura were separate antitrust markets).

continue to operate the acquired firm's stores under their prior store name. Technically, we identify mergers using the Trade Dimensions data by we identifying all instances where an incumbent firm begins operating stores that had previously been operated by a rival in a given market. We then searched the trade press and local newspapers to confirm that this observed change in store ownership was the result of either a horizontal merger or acquisition. For all but one of the mergers we study, we have been able to identify at least one press article identifying the merger.[26]

Our dataset contains price data for 357 different geographic regions (CBSAs), however, only 248 of the markets meet our inclusion criterion of having at least 10 quarters of data. Of these 248 markets, 27 experience at least one significant horizontal merger, 42 experience at least one significant entry event, and 64 experience at least one significant exit event. Many of the markets experiencing significant entry, exit, or a merger experience multiple changes in market structure during our sample period, or experience a change in market structure at the beginning or end of our sample period. Given our identification strategy, we cannot estimate the price effects of a merger for markets experiencing multiple changes in market structure within our sample period. When we limit attention to those markets that 1) experienced only one significant merger, and 2) experienced mergers in either 2007 or 2008, we are left with our estimation sample of 14 markets experiencing horizontal mergers.[27] Table 1 provides some information describing the markets affected by horizontal mergers, including the number of stores directly involved in the merger, the number of stores in the market, the number of firms

---

[26] We have been unable to find an article documenting the merger which took place in Fort Smith, Arkansas.

[27] While we include club stores in the market of firms we study, we did not observe any mergers involving club stores that met our inclusion criteria in the markets we examined during our time period. As noted earlier, most medium-sized and all large geographic markets experience some entry and exit during our sample period (Hanner et al. (2011)). As a result, the large markets affected by mergers also experience some entry and exit. However, as shown in Hanner et al. the aggregate effect of this entry and exit activity is much smaller than the changes in market structure caused by the mergers in the large markets studied here.

operating in the market prior to treatment, a short narrative describing each transaction, and an

rough estimate of market concentration in the broad geographic area affected by the merger.[28]

There is significant heterogeneity in the size and estimated market concentration of the markets

experiencing mergers. Our sample consists of a number of medium-sized U.S. markets, with less

than 100 retail outlets, and some massive markets, including metropolitan New York,

Philadelphia, and Detroit with hundreds of retail outlets. Over half of our merger sample

consists of highly concentrated grocery markets (with estimated HHIs greater than 2,500), while

the remaining markets are relatively unconcentrated. New York and Philadelphia, for example,

both have HHI's below 1,000. This variability in market concentration provides us with an

opportunity to determine if there is a systematic relationship between market concentration and

the price effects resulting from consummated mergers.

IV. Empirical Model and Results

The goal of our study is to determine how consumer prices are affected by changes in

market structure resulting from horizontal mergers within a retail market. The major issue faced

by any study attempting to measure the effect of a change in market structure on retail prices is

to develop a reasonable estimate of the counterfactual change in prices had the change not

occurred. Simply comparing the average prices in a market affected by a horizontal merger to

prices beforehand assumes this counterfactual change is zero, and this simple time difference

will be biased if something unrelated but concurrent in timing to the change in market structure

---

[28] We use the estimated grocery revenues of all club, supercenter, and supermarket retailers within the broad geographic regions affected by mergers in calculating market concentration (HHI). Our measure of market concentration would likely differ from that calculated by an antitrust agency in a merger investigation. An antitrust agency may define the product or geographic market differently and will have access to different revenue data (typically from subpoena responses rather than Trade Dimensions) to calculate market concentration. In particular, many of the geographic regions we are examining are quite large in size, possibly larger than the antitrust markets suggested by the *Horizontal Merger Guidelines*.

also affected prices. Grocery prices, particularly meat and produce, are highly volatile. An increase (decrease) in the price of some food items coincident with the market event being studied would bias a simple time difference estimator of the event's effect on prices upward (downward).

We use two methods to calculate merger price effects. The first method follows the literature and estimates merger price effects using a difference-in-difference estimator; that is, we identify merger price effects by comparing the change in prices in markets affected by mergers to presumably similar markets unaffected by the merger. For this approach to be valid, it must be the case that the change in price of the comparison markets closely approximates the counterfactual change in price that would have occurred in the market affected by the event had the event not occurred. To validate these results we examine how similar the merger and comparison markets are, and determine how robust the merger estimates are to changes in the comparison group used in estimation.

The second method estimates price effects using the synthetic control method suggest by Abadie et al. (2010). This is a data-driven technique that uses information on pre-merger prices and demographic characteristics to construct an explicit forecast of price for the counterfactual in the treatment market.

Difference-in-Difference Estimates

We first estimate price effects using the difference-in-difference estimation in equation (1) below, where the (log) of retailer i's price in market j in quarter t is regressed on a retailer/market specific fixed-effect (γ_{ij}), a time indicator to control for idiosyncratic factors affecting grocery prices in all markets in a given quarter (δ_t), an indicator set equal to one in the post-merger period for the market affected by treatment, and (in some specifications) controls for time-varying market specific factors (x_{ijt}) which may affect grocery pricing.

$$\log(p_{ijt}) = \gamma_{ij} + \delta_t + \theta(\text{Post-Event}_{ijt}) + \beta x_{ijt} + e_{ijt} \qquad (1)$$

Equation (1) is estimated separately for each merger event relative to the same comparison group, and standard errors are clustered by CBSA.

The first issue that arises in estimating equation (1) is how to measure grocery prices. We measure price by constructing a price index designed to measure the overall price of groceries offered by retailer at a point in time. We use the price index suggested by CCER. CCER's sample is constructed to correspond to a manager's food consumption bundle. To approximate this bundle, CCER has constructed expenditure weights using data extracted from the 2006 U.S. Consumer Expenditure Survey. We use these weights (w_k) to construct a price index for a retailer/market/quarter (p_{ijt}) as shown in equation (2) below

$$p_{ijt} = \sum_{k=1}^{26} w_k * p_{ijkt} \qquad (2)$$

where p_{ijkt} is the price of product k sold by retailer i in market j in time quarter t and w_k is the expenditure share associated with product k. We use this price index because it likely corresponds to the "price" consumers consider when choosing the grocery retailer to shop at in a time period. The literature has typically modeled the price that consumers consider in choosing a retailer as the price of the entire bundle of products they will purchase rather than the price of any single item in the bundle, see, e.g., Bliss (1988).[29]

---

[29] We have also considered treating the unit of observation as the price quote for a specific item, at a given retailer, in a market in a quarter; that is, the price of a product k (a 12 ounce box of corn flakes) sold by retailer i (Safeway) in market j (San Francisco) in quarter t (first quarter of 2007). The primary advantage of this approach is that there is much more data to estimate the pricing equation. When using this price measure we estimate a variant of equation (1) where the fixed-effect is redefined to correspond to a specific retailer/market/product (γ_{ijk}). This allows the mean price of each items to vary by both retailer and market. In this specification we assume the event being

We next must specify the timing of the event; that is, determine when we think the merger could begin having an effect on grocery pricing. To some extent, we are constrained by our data. While we can identify the year in which a merger took place in the Trade Dimensions data, we have been unable to identify precisely the quarter in which all of the mergers occurred.[30] To avoid contamination bias, we have dropped data corresponding to the year in which the event took place, so that the pre-event and post-event periods are clearly defined. For example, if we observe a merger took place in 2007, we drop data from 2007 from the regression analysis and define 2005 and 2006 as the pre-merger period and 2008 and 2009 as the post-merger period.

We now turn to the issue of identifying a credible comparison group. The ideal comparison group would consist of grocery markets experiencing demand and supply conditions similar to those experiencing mergers (in particular, experiencing similar pre-merger trends in pricing to the merger markets) that did not experience a large change in market structure. Markets that experienced important exit, entry, or horizontal mergers during our sample period are poor candidates for the comparison market, because prices in these markets may have been affected by changes in market structure. As discussed in the previous section, we consider two candidate sets of comparison markets. The first consists of 75 markets that did not experience a change in market structure as the result of entry, exit, or a horizontal merger during our sample period. The second consists of 117 markets that experienced no entry, exit or mergers that affected more than 2% of stores in a market. Table 2 presents demographic characteristics of the merger and comparison markets to examine how these markets are similar and different. The

---

studied affects all products sold by retailers in the market proportionately by an amount θ. As a practical matter, both price measures yield very similar estimated price effects. Because much of the grocery pricing literature suggests that consumers pick a retailer based on the price of the bundle of goods they will purchase at the retailer (rather than the price of any single item), we only present results in this paper using the price of the bundle.
[30] For the larger mergers we have been able to identify the dates the transactions closed, e.g., A&P's merger with Pathmark. For smaller events, such as the opening or closing of a store in a small CBSA, we have not been able to precisely identify each event date.

average market in the narrow comparison group is much smaller than the average merger market. The major cause of this difference is that all of the large U.S. markets experience some entry, exit, and or mergers by chain grocery retailers; that is, there are no major metropolitan areas in the narrow comparison group. When we weaken the requirement to include those markets that experience small levels of entry, exit, or horizontal mergers, the average market in the broader comparison group becomes much larger. However, because the merger sample consists of some of the largest U.S. metropolitan areas, the average market in the merger group is still much larger than the average market in the broader comparison group.

To address the concern that some markets in the comparison group may not be well matched to the treatment group, we estimate two additional specifications that limit the comparison group to regions experiencing similar pre-merger trending in prices to the merger city. To implement this we estimate a pre-merger price trend for each market in our data using equation (3), where for each market (j) we regress retailer i's (log) price on a retailer/market fixed-effect (γ_{ij}) and a time trend using only data from the pre-merger period.[31]

$$\log(p_{ijt}) = \gamma_{ij} + \alpha_j t + e_{ijt} \qquad (3)$$

Unfortunately, our ability to estimate the time trend in grocery prices is limited by our relatively short panel. For markets experiencing mergers in 2007 and 2008, we have only five and eight quarters of data, respectively, to estimate a region's pre-event trend in prices. As a result, our estimate of a region's time trend can be imprecise. Then for each treatment market we compare that treatment market's estimated time trend to that of each market in the comparison group, and

---

[31] Equation (3) is estimated once for each treatment market (with data restricted to that market's pre-event period). The equation is estimated twice for each comparison city using data from 2005 and 2006, and 2005, 2006, and 2007. When comparing a treatment region to a comparison region, we use the estimate the corresponds to the same estimation period. For example, in constructing a comparison group for New York (which experienced a merger in 2007) we use estimates of α_j for the comparison markets estimated with data from 2005 and 2006.

in most cases, only include those markets whose estimated time trend is within 0.005 of the treatment markets.[32] For example, prior to the merger of A&P and Pathmark in 2007, grocery prices in the New York CBSA were increasing at 1.025% a quarter $(\alpha_{\text{NewYork}} = 0.01025)$. We then limit New York's comparison group to those comparison markets where the trend in grocery prices is within the range of 0.5% and 1.525% per quarter.

We next formally test to determine if a given comparison market's time trend in the pre-merger period is statistically different for each merger/comparison market combination. Specifically, we estimate equation (4) using data on pre-merger prices for all retailers in one treatment market and one comparison group market, and we test whether the interaction of the time trend with an indicator for a retailer being in the merger market is different than zero; i.e., whether prices are trending significantly different from one another in the merger and comparison market.

$$\log p_{ijt} = a_{ij} + \alpha_1 t + \alpha_2 t * \text{MergerCity}_j + e_{ijt} \qquad (4)$$

The result of these tests appear in Table 3 where we conduct two-sided t-tests that $\alpha_2 = 0$ at the 5, 10, 15, and 20% significance levels. We see that most of the markets affected by mergers experience different pre-merger pricing trends than a significant fraction of the markets in the comparison group. As an additional specification check we limit the comparison group used in the difference-in-difference analysis to those markets whose price trends are not statistically different (at the 10% significance level) from the trend in the merger market.

Finally we highlight an important interpretation issue of our study. Our price index may over-estimate the price effects associated with mergers, because the price index is

---

[32] We require that the limited comparison group contain at least five regions. One merger market's (Albuquerque) pricing was trending differently enough from the regions in the comparison group that we had to increase the bounds to generate a control group containing at least five regions.

disproportionately composed of items that are especially sensitive to competition. Retailers

often pursue different pricing strategies for the different consumer products they sell. For

example, studies of grocery retailing have found that retailers are more likely to place "popular

products," those consumed by a large fraction of consumers and/or products that experience a

predictable seasonal demand spike, on sale than other grocery items (MacDonald (1998),

Chevalier et al. (2003), Hosken and Reiffen (2004b)). Retailers likely pursue this strategy

because offering low prices on commonly and frequently purchased products (the products

consumers are most informed about) is a cost-effective mechanism to communicate to consumers

a store's price level. Low prices on infrequently purchased items (about which consumers are

relatively uninformed) are less likely to increase a retailer's output, because consumers are

unlikely to respond to them (Lal and Matutes (1994), Hosken and Reiffen (2004b)). Ashenfelter

et al. (2006) report that the office supply retailer Staples pursued this pricing strategy. Staples

categorized products into four categories which varied in the sensitivity of the product's pricing

to competition.[33] The prices of frequently purchased items, such as copier paper or pens, were

adjusted much more in response to changes in competition (entry or exit of a close rival) than the

prices of less frequently purchased items (staplers). In measuring the price of the typical bundle

of office supplies purchased by a Staples' consumer, Ashenfelter et al. constructed a bundle of

products that contained products in each of the four categories weighted by the relative revenue

share of the category.

Unfortunately, in our study, we do not know exactly how pricing varies across the items

included in the CCER price index. We do, however, suspect that many of the products sampled

by CCER include items that are likely to be more sensitive to the level of retail competition than

the average product. By construction, the CCER pricing sample consists of commonly

---

[33] The categories were known as leadership, price sensitive, non-price sensitive, and invisible items.

purchased items, such as Corn Flakes, 2 liter bottles of Coca Cola, and meat items (ground beef, steak, and chicken), which are more likely to be offered on sale than the average supermarket product and are whose prices are more likely to be highly responsive to changes in competition.[34] As a result, it is likely that our price index will be more sensitive to changes in retail competition than an index that included all products sold by the grocery retailer (weighted appropriately by relative expenditures). Despite this shortcoming, our price index should correctly estimate the sign of the price effect of a given treatment on a retailer's pricing, and the *relative* size of the our estimated price effects should correspond to the relative change in a retailer's pricing; that is, where we estimate a large price effect, it is likely that a retailer's prices increased more.

Difference-in-Difference Results

Table 4 presents the empirical results for the difference-in-difference models estimated for those markets experiencing horizontal mergers. Each entry in Table 4 corresponds to the estimated price effect (θ from equation 1) when estimating equation (1) using data from one merger market and some or all of the regions in the broad control group.[35] The first column in each table corresponds to regressions estimated using only retailer/market fixed-effects and time indicators as controls. The second column includes variables that measure within-market expansion or contraction by incumbent supermarket and supercenter retailers as controls for other within-market changes in retail competition which may be contemporaneous with the event being studied.[36] The third column limits the comparison group to those markets with similar pre-

---

[34] See appendix A for a complete list of items contained in the price index.

[35] We have also estimated the difference-in-difference models using the more restrictive comparison group and have obtained very similar estimated price effects.

[36] The ratio of the number of stores opened (closed) by expanding (contracting) incumbent supermarket (supercenters) firms in the current year to the total number of stores operating in that market in the previous year.

event trends in pricing to the treatment group. The fourth column limits the comparison group to markets whose trends are not statistically different (at the 10% level) from the merger city.[37]

The difference-in-difference results for mergers are consistent with the price concentration hypothesis. While not all mergers in highly concentrated (unconcentrated) markets resulted in price increases (decreases), on average, those mergers generating the largest price increases take place in the most concentrated markets. We find that five mergers are estimated to have increased consumer prices by at least 2%, and that four of these mergers took place in highly concentrated markets (with estimated HHIs of more than 2500). Prices decreased by more than 2% following five mergers, and with one exception, these mergers took place in much less concentrated markets than those experiencing price increases. The remaining four mergers resulted in little change in consumer prices.

Some of our estimated price effects are very large in absolute value. As we noted previously, many of the items in our price index are likely to be more strongly affected by changes in the level of retail competition than a random item. As a result, the CCER bundle may overestimate the overall price effect of the merger. For example, while we estimate that the price of the CCER bundle fell by between 10-13% in San Francisco and San Jose following the purchase of Albertson's food by Save-Mart, we strongly suspect that the reduction in grocery prices for all grocery items would be considerably smaller. Unfortunately, we do not have access to information about how the prices in the CCER bundle relate to the prices of other (unobserved) items sold by retailers to extrapolate from our results to directly estimate how

---

[37] We have also estimated models including the prices of other retail goods sold by non-food retailers (a man's shirt, women's slacks, boy's pants and tennis balls) as was done by Basker and Noel (2009) and find that the inclusion of these variables has no effect on the estimated price effects. However, because these prices are missing for some market/time periods, the inclusion of these variables in the estimating equation causes us to drop some time periods from the estimation sample. To maximize the size of the estimation sample, we do not include these variables in the results presented in the paper.

much overall grocery prices changed following these mergers.[38] For this reason, we interpret our estimated price effects as being a relative measure of how much the overall price level changed as the result of a change in market structure. That is, we conclude that the Save-Mart/Albertson transaction in San Francisco and San Jose led to the relatively large price reductions, while the merger of A&P and Pathmark led to more modest price reductions in New York and Philadelphia.

Synthetic Control Groups

The difference-in-differences results presented in the previous section are robust to several regression specifications and comparison groups. This section further assesses the robustness of the empirical results to the choice of comparison group using the synthetic control group estimator developed by Abadie et al. (2010). The synthetic control method uses observed characteristics of geographic markets to construct a synthetic control price (defined to be a weighted average of a subset of the comparison group's prices) for each treatment (merger) market. For example, the best comparison price for Oklahoma City, Oklahoma is the sum of 0.20 times the price index of Providence, RI; 0.19 times the price index of Tampa, FL; 0.16 times the price index of Paducah, KY; 0.12 times the price index of Cedar City, UT; 0.10 times the price index of Tuscaloosa, AL; and smaller proportions of 10 additional CBSA or CSAs. For a given merger market, the optimal weights corresponding to each potential control market's price are determined using data on demographics and prices from the pre-merger period for each potential comparison market. We estimate the price effect of the merger by taking the difference between the observed post-merger price of the merger city and the price of the "synthetic control." Our synthetic control estimator is discussed below in more detail.

---

[38] To our knowledge, only one study, Ashenfelter et al. (2006), discussed above, has access to such data.

23

Implementation

Let $t = 1, \dots, T$ be the time periods covered by the data and let t_M be the period in which the merger of interest occurred. Define $i = 1$ to be the geographic market in which the merger occurred, and let $i = 2, \dots, I$ be the $I - 1$ potential comparison markets. P_{it} is the observed average price in market i at time t, and define $\widetilde{P_{it}}$ to be the average price that would obtain if no merger had occurred. The relationship between P_{it} and $\widetilde{P_{it}}$ in markets $(1, \dots, i, \dots, I)$ is given by

$$P_{it} = \widetilde{P_{it}} + \alpha_{it} D_{it} \qquad\qquad (4)$$

where

$$\begin{cases} D_{it} = 1 \; if \; i = 1 \; and \; t > t_M \\ \quad\; D_{it} = 0 \; otherwise. \end{cases}$$

The variable of interest, the effect of the merger on average prices, is α_{it} for periods $t = t_M + 1, \dots, T$. To construct an estimate of α_{1_t}, the unobserved $\widetilde{P_{1t}}$ are estimated for periods following the merger by taking the difference between the observed average price in market 1 and a weighted average of the average prices in the control markets. These weights are found by matching the observed attributes of control markets to the merger market in the pre-merger period. Specifically, we estimate the set of weights $w = (w_2, w_3, \dots, w_I)$ that minimize the difference between $\widetilde{P_{1t}}$ and $\sum_{i=2}^{I} w_i \widetilde{P_{it}}$ for periods $t = 1, \dots, t_M - 1$, where $\sum_{i=2}^{I} w_i \widetilde{P_{it}}$ is specified as a function of observed market attributes.[39] The weighted sum, $\sum_{i=2}^{I} w_i \widetilde{P_{it}}$, has the following form:

---

[39] Recall that we drop data from the year a merger took place. For example, in estimating the price effects of a merger that took place in 2007, the pre-merger period includes data from 2005 and 2006 and post-merger data from 2008 and 2009.

$$\sum_{i=2}^{I} w_i \tilde{P_{it}} = \sum_{i=2}^{I} w_i X_i + \sum_{i=2}^{I} \varepsilon_{it}, \qquad (5)$$

where each $k \times 1$ X_i vector includes market-specific attributes – population, population density, median per capita income, percentage of population that is black, percentage of population that is Hispanic, percentage of population below the poverty level, and price-levels – averaged across time periods 1 to $t_M - 1$, as well as the change in each of these variables from period 1 to period $t_M - 1$. The ε_{it} are idiosyncratic unobserved shocks to demand and or costs in market I at time t. The unknown parameters and weights in equation (5) are estimated by iteratively choosing the $w = (w_2, ..., w_I)$ and V that minimize

$$(X_1 - \sum_{i=2}^{I} w_i X_i)'V(X_1 - \sum_{i=2}^{I} w_i X_i), \qquad (6)$$

where V is a $k \times k$ symmetric positive semidefinite matrix.[40] The optimal weights, $w^* = (w_2^*, ..., w_I^*)$, are then used to estimate the desired $\tilde{P_{1t}}$ and α_{1t}.

We use Stata code developed by Abadie et al. (2010) to estimate the synthetic control model.[41] Abadie et al.'s program requires that there be a single time series for the treatment group being analyzed. Thus, we need to aggregate the data to the level of a market/quarter from a market/retailer/quarter. However, we cannot simply construct a simple average of the retailers' prices in a market, because not all retailers are observed in a market in every time period; that is, the composition of retailers observed in a market varies over time. Therefore, we construct a

---

[40] We begin each synthetic regression at three different initial V matrices. For each initial V, we employ a fully nested optimization routine that searches over all diagonal positive definite matrices V and weights w for the control that minimizes (6). Finally, we choose the control that produced the smallest value of (6) among the three starting V matrices.

[41] The Stata programs implementing the synthetic treatment estimator are available at: http://www.mit.edu/~jhainm/synthpage.html.

price index that controls for retailer/market effects. Specifically, we regress retailer i's (log) price in market j at time t on a retailer/market fixed-effect (α_{ij}) and a series of time indicators. We estimate these regressions at the retailer/market level.

$$\log(p_{ijt}) = \alpha_{ij} + \sum_t \delta_{jt} + e_{ijt} \tag{7}$$

The time indicator $\left(\delta_{jt}\right)$ from equation (7) estimates market *j*'s average price at time *t*, holding retailer effects constant. We use the estimated δ_{jt} as prices in the synthetic control group estimator.[42] Abadie et al.'s STATA programs also require a balanced panel. Hence, for a given merger, we limit the potential set of controls to comparison markets that report prices for each period reported by the merger market.

In most cases, the synthetic control appears to closely fit the treatment market in the pre-treatment period. Figure 1 provides a representative plot of Oklahoma City's actual price index and its synthetic control price pre- and post-merger.[43] Recall that to avoid contamination bias, the year the merger occurred – in this case 2007 – was excluded from the empirical analyses. Therfore, data from 2007 is also excluded from Figure 1. As can be seen in the figure, Oklahoma City's price index matches its synthetic control nearly perfectly in the pre-merger period (Q2-2005 thru Q3-2006), and then diverges noticeably post-merger (Q1-2008 thru Q3-2009).

Abadie et al. do not calculate conventional standard errors for the estimated effects of treatment. The authors argue that in aggregate studies (like ours) the most important source of uncertainty is not the estimated precision of the price change within a region (which is typically estimated with a high degree of precision) but in the uncertainty of the methodology itself. To

---

[42] Prices are all normalized relative to the first quarter of 2006 $\left(\delta_{j,Q_1\,2006} = 0 \text{ for all regions } j\right)$. All included treatment and comparison markets report a price in the first quarter of 2006.
[43] Similar figures are available for all of the markets studied in this paper upon request.

understand the importance of this uncertainty, the authors suggest that researchers conduct placebo studies to compare how the measured effect of treatment for the region that actually received treatment compares to the measured effect of treatment for those regions that (by assumption) did not receive treatment. We implement this methodology as follows. For every merger/comparison group combination, we treat each comparison region as if it was "treated" and calculate the average effect of treatment. This generates a distribution of up to 116 placebo treatment effects (one effect corresponding to each member of the comparison group). [44] We then rank these effects from smallest to largest and report the percentile corresponding to the estimated merger price effect. Table 5 presents the synthetic control estimates and the percentiles of the counterfactual pricing distribution generated by the placebo study in columns 3 and 4 respectively. For example, the estimated price effect of the supermarket merger in Oklahoma City is 6.2%. This price effect falls in the 94th percentile of the counterfactual pricing distribution; that is, 94% of the estimated price effects in the placebo group are smaller than the price effect for Oklahoma City.

To facilitate comparison of the synthetic control estimates to the difference-in-difference estimates, we have re-estimated the difference-in-difference model using the same data used in the synthetic control analysis (the market-level prices generated by equation 7). We also generate an analogous measure of where the difference-in-difference estimate falls in the counterfactual distribution. For each year in which a merger event can take place (2007 or 2008), we estimate how much the price changed following that year for each comparison market and market that experienced a merger in that year as in equation 8 below.

$$\log(p_{ijt}) = \gamma_{ij} + \theta_j (\text{Post-Event}_{ijt}) + e_{ijt} \qquad (8)$$

---

[44] Some of the initial 117 comparison cities do not have complete panels of data and had to be dropped from the synthetic control analysis.

We then sort the estimated price effects (θ_j) from smallest to largest for the comparison group and record which percentile a given merger market's estimated price effect corresponds to. Columns 1 and 2 of Table 5 contain the estimated price effect and the percentile of the counterfactual pricing distribution to which a price effect corresponds to. For example, the difference-in-difference model estimates the price effect of the merger in Oklahoma City increased price by 7%. That price effect was larger than 93% of the price changes taking place in the comparison group following the merger.

The difference-in-difference estimates in Table 5 are very similar to those estimated with retailer/market level data (Table 4) suggesting that the data aggregation used in equation (7) does not result in a meaningful change in our estimated price effects. While the difference-in-difference and synthetic control models estimates are not identical, they are very similar both qualitatively and quantitatively. In only one case (Fort Wayne, IN) is the sign of the estimated price effect of the merger materially impacted by the choice of estimation method, and then only modestly – the estimated price effect associated with the merger in Fort Wayne varies between zero and -1% when using the various difference-in-difference estimators and is roughly -3% when using the synthetic control group. The robustness of the estimated merger price effects to both model specification and choice of control group suggests that mergers are likely exogenous to the time path of prices within the market affected by the merger; that is, the failure to explicitly control for the potential endogeneity of mergers does not appear to affect the magnitude of the estimated price effects.

It is also important to compare the estimates of precision (standard errors) from the difference-in-difference results (Table 4) to the percentiles of the counterfactual distribution (columns 3 and 4 of Table 5). The difference-in-difference estimates should be interpreted as the

28

change in grocery prices post-merger in the market directly affected by the merger relative to the *mean* change in price in the comparison group. As Abadie et al. note, in most aggregate studies these estimates tend to be very precise, and our study is no exception. Virtually all of the standard errors in Table 4 are less than 0.5%. From this we can conclude that the mean change in price in a merger market is different than the mean change in price in the comparison group even for small changes in price (less than 2%). However, the results from the placebo study show that many markets in the comparison groups also experience changes in price similar to those of the treatment markets. For example, roughly 19% of the comparison markets experience reductions in price at least as large as those experienced by Detroit (column 2 Table 4). The results of the placebo studies for both the difference-in-difference and synthetic control estimates show that relatively small estimated price effects (under 2% in absolute value) are not uncommon in the comparison group. As a result, we cannot be confident that relatively small estimated price effects were caused by the merger rather than other factors.

V. Conclusion

Antitrust enforcement agencies must decide how many competitors are necessary to maintain competition within a market. The answer to this question depends on market specific supply and demand factors such as the degree of product differentiation, ease of entry and expansion, and the model of competition that best fits the industry. By examining a relatively large number of mergers taking place in the same industry that occurred at roughly the same time we can draw some conclusions about how changes in market structure caused by a merger affect prices. Despite the relative ease of entry and expansion and low aggregate profit margins, we find evidence that horizontal mergers in the supermarket industry can result in significant increases in consumer prices and thereby harm consumers. The mergers that result in higher consumer prices are largely those that we would expect, *a priori*, to be potentially competitively harmful. When market concentration increases in highly concentrated markets as the result of a horizontal merger, we frequently -- but not always -- observe significant increases in grocery prices. Our results are consistent with the broader merger retrospective literature: mergers on the enforcement margin are, on average, associated with price increases.

Because the literature has focused on estimating the price effects of mergers on the enforcement margin, there is little empirical evidence describing how presumably benign mergers affect consumer prices. Our study helps fill this gap. We find that mergers in unconcentrated or moderately concentrated markets grocery mergers are often associated with reductions in consumer prices. This result supports the presumption that competitively benign mergers can confer significant efficiencies that are passed on to consumer in the form of lower prices. Overall, our study's findings support the use of market concentration as a screen (as employed by the *Horizontal Merger Guidelines*) to aid antitrust agencies in efficiently deploying scarce enforcement resources.

We also find that there is no single price effect resulting from a merger. While the estimated price effect of each merger we examine is robust to model specification and estimation technique, the estimated price effects vary dramatically across mergers, even mergers resulting in similar changes in market concentration. Because of this, we advocate estimating price effects separately by market and transaction where sufficient data is available, rather than estimating a single overall price effect. By examining the empirical distribution of merger price effects we can learn how frequently potentially problematic mergers result in increased consumer prices, or how frequently likely benign mergers result in lower or unchanged consumer prices.

References

Abadie, Alberto, Diamond, Alexis, and Jens Hainmueller. 2010. "Synthetic Control Methods for Comparative Case Studies: Estimating the Effect of California's Tobacco Control Program," *Journal of the American Statistical Association* 105, 493-505.

Ashenfelter, Orley, Ashmore, David, Baker, Jonathan, Gleason, Suzanne, and Daniel Hosken. 2006. "Empirical Methods in Merger Analysis: Econometric Analysis of Pricing in FTC v. Staples," *International Journal of The Economics of Business* 13(2), 265-279.

Ashenfelter, Orley, Daniel Hosken, and Matthew Weinberg. 2009. "Generating Evidence to Guide Merger Enforcement." *Competition Policy International* 5(1), 67-85

Basker, Emek and Michael Noel. 2009. "The Evolving Food Chain: Competitive Effects of Wal-Mart's Entry into the Supermarket Industry," *Journal of Economics and Management Strategy* 18 (4), 977-1009

Bliss, Christopher. 1988. "A Theory of Retail Pricing." *Journal of Industrial Economics* 36 (4), 375-391

Bresnahan Timothy and Peter Reiss. 1990. "Entry in Monopoly Markets," *Review of Economic Studies* 57, 531-553

---- and ---. 1991. "Entry and Competition in Concentrated Markets," *Journal of Political Economy* 99 (5), 977-1009

Bronnenberg, Bart J., Michael W. Kruger, and Carl F. Mela. 2008. "The IRI Marketing Data Set." *Marketing Science* 27 (4), 745-748

Carlton, Dennis W. 2009. "Why We Need to Measure the Effect of Merger Policy and How to Do It." *Competition Policy International* 5 (1), 87-100

Chevalier, Judith A., Anil K. Kashyap, and Peter E. Rossi. 2003. "Why Don't Prices Rise during Periods of Peak Demand? Evidence from Scanner Data." *American Economic Review* 93 (1), 15-37

Courtemanche, Charles and Art Carden. 2011. "Competing Costco and Sam's Club: Warehouse Club Entry and Grocery Prices." *NBER Working Paper 17220*

Dafny, Leemore. 2009. "Estimation and Identification of Merger Effects: An Application to Hospital Mergers." *Journal of Law and Economics* 52 (3), 523-550

Davis, David. 2010. "Prices, Promotions, and Supermarket Mergers," *Journal of Agricultural and Food Industrial Organization* 8 (1), Article 8

Demsetz, Harold. 1973. "Industry Structure, Market Rivalry, and Public Policy," *Journal of Law and Economics*, 16 (1), 1-9

Evans, William, Froeb, Luke, and Greg Werden. 1993. "Endogeneity in the Concentration-Price Relationship: Causes, Consequences, and Cures," *Journal of Industrial Economics*, 41 (4) ,431-438

Federal Trade Commission (FTC). 2008. *Horizontal Merger Investigation Data Fiscal Years 1996-2007*. Washington, DC: FTC

----. 2010. "FTC Challenges A&P's Proposed Acquisition of Pathmark Supermarkets," available at: http://www.ftc.gov/opa/2007/11/pathwork.shtm.

Hanner, Daniel, Hosken, Daniel, Olson, Luke, and Loren Smith. 2011. "Dynamics in a Mature Industry: Entry, Exit, and Growth of Big-Box Grocery Retailers," *Federal Trade Commission Bureau of Economics Working Paper 308*

Hausman, Jerry and Ephraim Liebtag. 2007. "Consumer Benefits from Increased Competition in Shopping Outlets: Measuring the Effect of Wal-Mart," *Journal of Applied Econometrics* 22 (7), 1157-77

Hosken, Daniel, and David Reiffen. 2004a. "Patterns of Retail Price Variation." *RAND Journal of Economics* 35 (1), 128-146

----, and----. 2004b. "How Retailers Determine Which Products Should Go on Sale: Evidence from Store-Level Data." *Journal of Consumer Policy* 27 (2), 141-177

Huang, Kun and Kyle Stiegert. 2009. "Evaluating a Supermarket Merger Event: The Case of Copps and Kohl's in Madison WI," *FSRG Monograph Series, #21*

Hunter, Graeme, Leonard, Gregory, and Steven Olley. 2008. "Merger Retrospective Studies: A Review," *Antitrust* 23 34-41

Kim, E. and Vijay Singal. 1993. "Mergers and Market Power: Evidence from the Airline Industry." *American Economic Review* 83, 549-569.

Lal, Rajiv, and Carmen Matutes. 1994. "Retail Pricing and Advertising Strategies." *Journal Of Business* 67 (3), 345-370.

MacDonald, James M. 2000. "Demand, Information, and Competition: Why Do Food Prices Fall at Seasonal Demand Peaks?" *Journal of Industrial Economics* 48 (1), 27-45.

Matsa, David A. 2011. "Competition and Product Quality in the Supermarket Industry." *Quarterly Journal of Economics* 126 (3),1539-1591.

Nevo, Aviv and Michael Whinston. 2010. "Taking the Dogma out of Econometrics: Structural Modeling and Credible Inference," *Journal of Economic Perspectives* 24 (2), 69-81

Pautler, Paul. 2003. "Evidence on Mergers and Acquisitions." *Antitrust Bulletin* 48, 119-207.

Prager, Robin and Timothy Hannan. 1998. "Do Substantial Horizontal Mergers Generate Significant Price Effects? Evidence from the Banking Industry." *Journal of Industrial Economics* 46, 433-452

Silvia, Louis and Christopher Taylor. 2009. "Petroleum Mergers and Competition in the Northeast United States," *forthcoming International Journal of the Economics of Business.*

U.S. Department of Justice (DOJ) and FTC. 2010. *Horizontal Merger Guidelines.* Washington, DC: DOJ and FTC

Weinberg, Matthew. 2008. "The Price Effects of Horizontal Mergers," *Journal of Competition Law and Economics*, 4 (2), 433-447

Table 1: Description of Mergers Studied

Market	Merger Year	Merger Description	Acquiring Firm		Aquired Firm		Pre-Merger Firms In Market		Stores	Market Merger Revenue HHI	Change in HHI
			Stores	Revenue Share	Stores	Revenue Share	Chains	Independents			
Albuquerque, NM	2007	Albertsons buys 8 Raleys stores, 6 continue to operate; more stores in purchase, Raleys continued operation in N. Nevada and N. California.	10	0.09	8	0.06	7	14	72	3251	110
Detroit-Warren-Livonia, MI	2007	Kroger acquires roughly 20 Farmer Jack Supermarket locations from Great A & P Tea Co.	73	0.15	63	0.14	19	171	409	1260	412
Evansville, IN-KY	2008	Houchens Industries bought all Buehler Foods locations including 11 stores here.	5	0.07	11	0.13	8	9	47	3331	172
Fort Smith, AR-OK	2007	C V Foodliner buys 7 stores from CVM Inc.	10	0.08	7	0.06	4	7	42	5278	99
Fort Wayne, IN	2007	Kroger buys 11 stores from SuperValu Inc.	7	0.10	13	0.15	6	11	40	2943	313
Fresno, CA	2007	Save Mart Super Markets buys 5 stores from Albertsons.	24	0.36	5	0.06	11	34	86	1705	412
Muskogee, OK	2007	Assoc Wholesale Grocers Inc buys one store from Albertsons	3	0.13	1	0.08	5	3	11	3375	226
New Orleans-Metairie-Kenner, LA	2007	Rouse Enterprises buys 15 stores from Great A & P Tea Co	4	0.02	18	0.12	7	43	109	3462	57
New York-Northern New Jersey-Long Island, NY-NJ-PA	2007	Great A & P Tea Co buys 111 stores from Pathmark.	197	0.13	112	0.09	69	769	1755	597	222
Oklahoma City, OK	2007	Assoc Wholesale Grocers Inc buys 12 stores from Albertsons	13	0.04	12	0.06	11	24	113	3961	46
Philadelphia-Camden-Wilmington, PA-NJ-DE-MD	2007	Great A & P Tea Co buys 26 stores from Pathmark;.	38	0.07	26	0.05	33	96	452	817	72

Table 1: Description of Mergers Studied

Market	Merger Year	Merger Description	Aquiring Firm		Aquired Firm		Pre-Merger Firms In Market		Market		
			Stores	Revenue Share	Stores	Revenue Share	Chains	Independents	Stores	Merger Revenue HHI	Change in HHI
San Francisco-Oakland-Fremont, CA	2007	Save Mart Super Markets buys 42 stores from Albertsons.	13	0.05	42	0.11	23	73	317	2152	98
San Jose-Sunnyvale-Santa Clara, CA	2007	Save Mart Super Markets buys 8 stores from Albertsons.	8	0.06	19	0.11	21	27	145	1729	134
Topeka, KS	2008	Kroger buys 3 stores from Assoc Wholesale Grocers Inc.	7	0.27	6	0.11	4	11	30	3572	597

Table 2: Market Characteristics by Market Type Prior to Treatment

Market Characteristics	Market Type		
	Narrow Comparison*	Broad Comparison**	Merger
Price Index	2.26	2.27	2.59
	0.40	0.43	0.56
Price of Boy's Jeans	19.40	19.28	20.16
	3.91	3.87	3.81
Price of Men's Dress Shirt	26.43	25.67	30.32
	5.88	4.98	5.79
Price of Tennis Balls	2.34	2.32	2.37
	0.57	0.49	0.64
Price of Women Slacks	28.74	28.61	30.83
	6.47	6.88	7.67
Total Weekly Supermarket Revenue (thousands)	9,459	30,481	71,893
	18,050	48,303	111,037
Market Concentration (HHI)	3,368	2,914	2,334
	1,211	1,195	1,104
Proportional Growth of Incumbent Supercenter Firms	0.012	0.024	0.007
	0.029	0.010	0.004
Proportional Growth of Incumbent Supermarket Firms	0.007	0.020	0.013
	0.017	0.011	0.009
Proportional Contraction of Incumbent Supermarket Firms	0.009	0.022	0.030
	0.020	0.012	0.024
Median Household Income	41,087	44,043	47,898
	7,629	8,324	12,313
Total Population Under the Age of 19	84,891	283,256	779,964
	158,261	496,139	1,308,433
Population	299,437	1,002,184	2,889,977
	584,330	1,707,585	4,929,187
Percentage of Population in Poverty	0.148	0.137	0.137
	0.060	0.052	0.038
Percentage of Population African American	0.075	0.101	0.123
	0.100	0.105	0.099
Percentage of Population Hispanic	0.138	0.134	0.145
	0.197	0.175	0.150
Number of Markets in Group	75	117	14

The price statistics all correspond to the premerger time period for merger markets. Prices come from the first year of available data (either 2005 or 2006). All other statistics are calculated using 2005 measures.

*The narrow comparison group contains markets that do not experience entry, exit or a horizontal merger during the sample period (2005-2009).

*The broad comparison group contrains markets that do not experience any one entry, exit, or horizontal merger that affects more than 2% of stores in a market.

Table 3: Proportion of Control Cities Whose Prices Trend Pre-Merger Statistically Significantly Differently than the Merger City

Merger Market	Confidence Level of Test			
	p-value<.05	p-value<.1	p-value<.15	p-value<.2
Albuquerque	0.74	0.88	0.91	0.93
Detroit	0.02	0.05	0.08	0.11
Evansville	0.03	0.05	0.09	0.09
FortSmith	0.26	0.35	0.41	0.49
FortWayne	0.32	0.46	0.54	0.59
Fresno	0.19	0.28	0.35	0.41
Muskogee	0.02	0.03	0.07	0.08
NewOrleans	0.11	0.14	0.22	0.29
NewYork	0.10	0.18	0.27	0.36
OklahomaCity	0.26	0.35	0.39	0.46
Philadelphia	0.19	0.26	0.33	0.37
SanFrancisco	0.20	0.32	0.34	0.37
SanJose	0.13	0.21	0.27	0.32
Topeka	0.09	0.09	0.18	0.23

Table 4: Estimated Effects of Mergers on Price: Difference-in-Difference

Region	1	2	3	4
Albuquerque	-0.0316	-0.0327	-0.0532	-0.0441
	(0.00357)	(0.00416)	(0.0126)	(0.0101)
Detroit	-0.0272	-0.0273	-0.026	-0.0274
	(0.00361)	(0.00406)	(0.00665)	(0.00380)
Evansville	0.0191	0.0192	0.0188	0.0189
	(0.00348)	(0.00364)	(0.00506)	(0.00341)
Fort Smith	0.0358	0.0359	0.0356	0.0388
	(0.00344)	(0.00362)	(0.00746)	(0.00486)
Fort Wayne	-0.0112	-0.0111	-0.0108	-0.0129
	(0.00367)	(0.00373)	(0.0115)	(0.00448)
Fresno	0.0421	0.0423	0.0404	0.0441
	(0.00352)	(0.00390)	(0.00717)	(0.00450)
Muskogee	-0.000405	-0.000236	-0.000752	-0.000438
	(0.00344)	(0.00360)	(0.00732)	(0.00354)
New Orleans	0.03	0.0305	0.0296	0.0299
	(0.00344)	(0.00457)	(0.00732)	(0.00382)
New York	-0.0182	-0.018	-0.0152	-0.0177
	(0.00350)	(0.00365)	(0.00831)	(0.00402)
Oklahoma City	0.0582	0.0573	0.0648	0.0611
	(0.00345)	(0.00451)	(0.00785)	(0.00486)
Philadelphia	-0.0437	-0.0425	-0.0476	-0.0438
	(0.00345)	(0.00443)	(0.00458)	(0.00393)
San Francisco	-0.133	-0.133	-0.135	-0.134
	(0.00347)	(0.00467)	(0.00411)	(0.00399)
San Jose	-0.105	-0.107	-0.104	-0.105
	(0.00342)	(0.00542)	(0.00635)	(0.00378)
Topeka	0.0869	0.0874	0.0929	0.087
	(0.00342)	(0.00384)	(0.00540)	(0.00346)
Specification				
Market/Retailer Fixed-Effects	x	x	x	x
Quarter Indicators	x	x	x	x
Broad Comparison Group	x	x	x	x
Measures of within market expansion or contraction by incumbent retailers.		x		
Limit comparison to those with similar pre-merger trending			x	
Limit comparison group to markets where pre-merger trending is not statistically different (at 0.1 level) than merger region.				x

Standard errors (in parentheses) are clustered by region.

Dependent variable is the log of a retailer's price index in a region/quarter.

Table 5: Estimated Price Effects Mergers
Comparison of Difference-in-Difference and Synthetic Control Estimates

Merger Market	Pre-Merger HHI	Difference-in-Difference		Synthetic Control	
		Coefficient	Percentile Of Counterfactual Distribution	Coefficient	Percentile Of Counterfactual Distribution
Albuquerque	3251	-0.035	0.10	-0.026	0.27
Detroit	1260	-0.020	0.19	-0.053	0.14
Evansville	3331	0.013	0.54	0.006	0.53
Fort Smith	5278	0.048	0.84	0.065	0.94
Fort Wayne	2943	-0.001	0.56	-0.032	0.20
Fresno	1705	0.054	0.89	0.040	0.88
Muskogee	3375	0.010	0.47	-0.007	0.51
New Orleans	3462	0.035	0.75	0.019	0.75
New York	597	-0.009	0.32	-0.017	0.40
Oklahoma City	3961	0.070	0.93	0.062	0.94
Philadelphia	817	-0.035	0.11	-0.040	0.17
San Francisco	2152	-0.117	0.03	-0.115	0.04
San Jose	1729	-0.095	0.03	-0.078	0.09
Topeka	3572	0.077	0.96	0.060	0.92

Note: The difference-in-difference models include time indicators and market fixed-effects.

Appendix Table 1: Items in Grocery Bundle

Product	Expenditure weight	Product Description
T-bone Steak	0.031121	Price per pound
Ground Beef or Hamburger	0.031121	Price per pound, lowest price, min 80% lean
Sausage	0.03751	Price per pound, Jimmy Dean or Owens Brand, 100% pork
Frying Chicken	0.03648	Price per pound, whole fryer
Chunk Light Tuna	0.035243	6.0 oz can, Starkist or Chicken of the Sea
Whole Milk	0.034522	Half-Gallon Carton
Eggs	0.008141	One dozen, Grade A large
margarine	0.004288	One Pound, Cubes, Blue Bonnet or Parkay
Parmesan Cheese, grated	0.065746	8 oz. cannister, Kraft brand
Potatoes	0.030524	10 lb., white or red
Bananas	0.056884	Price per pound
Iceberg Lettuce	0.026154	Head, approximately 1.25 pounds
Bread, White	0.08512	24 oz loaf, lowest price, or prorated 24 oz. equivalent, lowest price
Fresh Orange juice	0.016255	64 oz (1.89 liters) Tropicana or Florida Natural Brand
Coffee, vacuum-packed	0.036501	11.5 oz. can, Maxwell House, Hillse Brothers, or Folgers
Sugar	0.03514	4 pound sack, cane or beet, lowest price
Corn Flakes	0.038438	18 oz., Kelloggs's or Post Toasties
Sweet Peas	0.012675	15-15.25 oz. can, Del Monte or Green Giant
Peaches	0.013836	29 ounce can , Hunts, Del Monte, Libby's, or Lady Alberta
Facial Tissues	0.051628	200-count box, Kleenex Brand
Dishwashing Powder	0.051628	75 oz. Cascade dishwashing powder
Shortening	0.017765	3 pound can, all vegetable, Crisco brand
Frozen Meal	0.099643	8 to 10 oz., frozen chicken entrée, Health Choice or Lean Cuisine brand
Frozen Corn	0.012675	16 oz., whole kernel, lowest price
Potato Chips	0.078015	12 oz. plain regular potato chips
Soft Drink	0.052947	2 liter Coca Cola excluding any deposit

Appendix Table 2: List Of Broad Comparison Group Cities

Americus, GA	Flagstaff, AZ	Odessa, TX
Ames, IA	Gainesville, FL	Omaha-Council Bluffs, NE-IA
Atlanta-Sandy Springs-Marietta, GA	Garden City, KS	Orlando-Kissimmee, FL
Austin-Round Rock, TX	Grand Junction, CO	Paducah, KY-IL
Bakersfield, CA	Greenville-Mauldin-Easley, SC	Palestine, TX
Baltimore-Towson, MD	Hartford-West Hartford-East Hartford, CT	Phoenix-Mesa-Scottsdale, AZ
Beaumont-Port Arthur, TX	Hays, KS	Pittsburgh, PA
Bellingham, WA	Hickory-Lenoir-Morganton, NC	Portland-Vancouver-Beaverton, OR-WA
Boise City-Nampa, ID	Hot Springs, AR	Prescott, AZ
Boston-Cambridge-Quincy, MA-NH	Houston-Sugar Land-Baytown, TX	Providence-New Bedford-Fall River, RI-MA
Bradenton-Sarasota-Venice, FL	Idaho Falls, ID	Pueblo, CO
Bridgeport-Stamford-Norwalk, CT	Indiana, PA	Punta Gorda, FL
Brownsville-Harlingen, TX	Indianapolis-Carmel, IN	Quincy, IL-MO
Burlington, IA-IL	Ithaca, NY	Raleigh-Cary, NC
Carlsbad-Artesia, NM	Jefferson City, MO	Richmond, VA
Cedar City, UT	Kansas City, MO-KS	Riverside-San Bernardino-Ontario, CA
Champaign-Urbana, IL	Kennewick-Pasco-Richland, WA	Salt Lake City, UT
Charleston, WV	Kodiak, AK	San Angelo, TX
Charleston-North Charleston-Summerville, SC	Lafayette, IN	San Antonio, TX
Charlottesville, VA	Lake Charles, LA	Seattle-Tacoma-Bellevue, WA
Cincinnati-Middletown, OH-KY-IN	Lake Havasu City-Kingman, AZ	Sheboygan, WI
Columbia, MO	Lancaster, PA	Shreveport-Bossier City, LA
Columbus, OH	Laramie, WY	Springfield, MO
Corpus Christi, TX	Las Cruces, NM	St. Cloud, MN
Dallas-Fort Worth-Arlington, TX	Las Vegas-Paradise, NV	St. George, UT
Danville, IL	Lima, OH	St. Louis, MO-IL
Dayton, OH	Little Rock-North Little Rock-Conway, AR	Tampa-St. Petersburg-Clearwater, FL
Decatur, IL	Los Angeles-Long Beach-Santa Ana, CA	Tucson, AZ
Denver-Aurora-Broomfield, CO	Louisville/Jefferson County, KY-IN	Tuscaloosa, AL
Des Moines-West Des Moines, IA	Mason City, IA	Twin Falls, ID
Dodge City, KS	McAllen-Edinburg-Mission, TX	Tyler, TX
Dubuque, IA	Memphis, TN-MS-AR	Valdosta, GA
Durham-Chapel Hill, NC	Miami-Fort Lauderdale-Pompano Beach, FL	Virginia Beach-Norfolk-Newport News, VA-NC
Dyersburg, TN	Mobile, AL	Washington-Arlington-Alexandria, DC-VA-MD-WV
Erie, PA	Morristown, TN	Waterloo-Cedar Falls, IA
Fairbanks, AK	Nashville-Davidson--Murfreesboro--Franklin, TN	Wausau, WI
Fargo, ND-MN	New Haven-Milford, CT	Wilmington, NC
Farmington, NM	Gunnison CO	Worcester, MA
Findlay, OH	Norwich-New London, CT	Yuma, AZ

www.ingramcontent.com/pod-product-compliance
Lightning Source LLC
Chambersburg PA
CBHW081238170526
45165CB00009B/3101